Libe-rated

A collection of heartfelt poems

Anaa

Made with ❤ on the BookLeaf Publishing Platform
www.bookleafpub.in
www.bookleafpub.com

Dedication

To Plum

Preface

Poetry has always been my way of making sense of the world—its beauty, its chaos, and the emotions that flow through us all. This collection, Libe-rated, was born out of quiet moments of introspection, fleeting encounters, and the rhythm of life itself.

Each poem is a piece of my journey, reflecting love, loss, hope, and renewal. Inspired by nature, human connection, and the simple yet profound experiences of everyday life, these verses aim to resonate with the reader's emotions and memories.

As you turn these pages, I invite you to wander through my words, to find yourself in them, and to let the poetry speak to you in its way. May these poems be a companion in your solitude, a spark of thought, or a whisper of comfort.

Acknowledgements

To the readers—thank you for allowing my words to find a home in your hearts.
And to the moments and people who helped me feel what I write.

1. Unbound

If it were just listening,
I'd call it attention.
If it were just longing,
I'd call it tension.

But it spilled beyond rivers,
wandered past roads,
a quiet tremor
where apprehension grows.

Was it luck?
Or was it affection—
this untamed flight,
this sweet defection?

Away from the world,
not a care, not a trace,
no weight, no tether,
just light and space.

Nothing to hold,
nothing to bind—

only the wind,
only the mind.

2. In the Shadow

In the hush beneath this tree,
or the quiet of his chin,
I forget the weight of undone things,
the ticking hands, the waiting strings.

The breeze runs wild within my veins,
like whispers steeped in coffee rains.
A fleeting ease, a tethered drift—
a moment held, a soul adrift.

But what if shade and shelter fade?
What if the hush is torn away?
Will I still be,
or only the ache of missing it?

3. Edge of Air

I stand on the brink,
where the world dissolves,
where echoes fade
and nothing evolves.

No tether of sorrow,
no shimmer of bliss,
no weight of longing,
no past to reminisce.

Not love, not loss,
not joy, not pain—
just open sky,
just quiet rain.

No name, no face,
no fate to obey—
only the wind
to carry me away.

4. Ghostlight

It was love,
or something close—
a slow collapse,
a beautiful wreck.

Your words, sugar-laced venom,
held me tight,
soft enough to keep me,
sharp enough to cut.

I called it passion,
called it fate—
but love shouldn't
feel like drowning.

Now, on the edge,
where your shadow fades,
I taste the air—
clear, electric, mine.

Maybe falling out
is just the glow returning.

5. "The Weight I Carry Quietly"

From the choices I make, a tremble is born,
A whisper of worry, soft yet worn.
Is it my roots, the way I was raised,
To be the "good one," forever praised?

Or is it the echoes of rooms once loud,
Where love got lost beneath the cloud
Of fights and silence, sharp and cold—
I learned to mend what I couldn't hold.

I only wish for joy to stay,
For smiles to linger, not drift away.
Let no heart break because I'm gone,
Let no tear fall when I move on.

And still—away, I feel so free,
Like guilt released its grip on me.
Is that wrong? To crave my peace?
To let the noise inside me cease?

I walk a line both thin and wide,
With love ahead and fear beside.

But still I walk, not just to flee—
But to find the space to finally *be*.

6. My Revolt

I am done with choosing just to fit—
Done with dimming my fire bit by bit.
Love will not chain me in sweet disguise,
I see too clear through well-dressed lies.

I won't bow to life's ticking plan,
I wasn't born to be a "yes" woman/man.
Let others chase their nine-to-five,
I crave the kind of wild that's alive.

No more nodding in family halls,
Wearing masks behind polite walls.
I love who I love, I walk my way—
And I won't apologize for straying astray.

Let the world call me lost or bold,
Let them scoff while I break the mold.
This freedom burns, this path is mine—
Untamed, unowned, by pure design.

I don't ask blessings, don't seek their praise,
I'm building a life they can't appraise.

No more pretending, no more "should"—
I choose *me* now. And it feels good.

7. No edits, No noise

Today,
I unwrite the story I told myself
about what I *should* be.

I forgive the girl
who thought suffering was the path to meaning.
I hold the woman
who chased freedom
but feared what she'd find without the chains.

This is not escape.
This is return.
To breath,
to softness,
to truth
without armor.

I am not running anymore.
I am resting
in the wreckage
of who I no longer need to be.

And in that stillness—
I begin.

8. Unearned Life

I want something smaller.
Softer.
Real.

Give me mornings without alarms.
Laughter that isn't proof of anything.
Eyes that don't measure,
hands that don't grip.

I want to sit with trees
and remember how it felt
before I knew what success was.
Before I learned to pretend.

There is a girl in me—
barefoot,
grass-stained,
untouched by needing to be "someone."

And she is waiting.
Not for applause,
but for stillness.
For sky.

I think I'll meet her there,
where the game ends,
and life—
sweet, ridiculous,
unearned life—
begins again.

9. The Flower Knows

The flower never asks
how much time remains.

It does not consult the sun's arc,
nor plead with the soil
for permission to arrive.

It blooms
only when it's ready—
slow, unapologetic,
a secret unfolding
for no one but itself.

Its beauty is not measured
by duration.
It opens.
It lives.
It lets go.

And even in the falling,
there is grace.

No voice declares it late.

No wind scolds the petal
for how it loosened its grip.

The flower knows—
that time is not a master,
but a passing breeze.

And so it leans
into the light
once more,
then disappears—
gently,
as if it had always
belonged to the air.

10. Final Freedom

Wake before the sun—
glow with purpose,
swallow your hunger,
both literal and metaphorical.

Smile like you've won
a race you never entered.
Post light.
Hide the burn.

Speak softly.
But only when spoken to.
Rise.
But make it elegant.

Collect milestones—
degrees, rings,
followers,
burnout.

They will clap
as you disappear

into curated peace,
one perfect filtered frame at a time.

Then,
when you've smiled long enough,
shrunk gracefully,
bled invisibly—

you may die.

Softly.
Beautifully.
Without complaint.

And they will say,
"She did it all."
As if that was ever
a life.

11. Returning

not broken—
only paused,
mid-breath
mid-becoming

the ache wasn't ruin,
only weight
carried too long
without asking why

light didn't rescue—
it remembered
the way back
through
you

no fixing
just
returning
to the self
that always
was

12. Vinyl Freedom

needle drops—
and suddenly
hips remember
what stillness forgot

snap of snare,
sugar in the swing,
velvet croon
unbuttoning the weight
of now

no overthinking
just jukebox joy,
rebellion in rhythm
freedom in falsetto

each note a time machine
to somewhere
never lived,
but always known

a place
where hearts
sway without shame

and
every beat
is permission

to feel
to move
to *be*

13. She Grew Quiet Among Leaves

She no longer asks the world
to be loud with meaning.

Now, she learns from green things—
how to rise without force,
how to stay rooted in stillness,
how to open
only when the sun says so.

I am her heart,
and I have seen
how the garden inside her
grows softer
with every leaf she tends.

She waters in silence,
and silence answers.

Peace does not shout—
it blooms.

14. Perhaps

Little one,
do not fear the stretch of day—
like I stretch my clouds so high,
let your heart unfold
in quiet grace.

For growth comes not with haste,
but in the gentle turning
of the earth beneath your feet,
and in the whispered light
that graces the morning's brow.

The storm shall come—
but know, as I,
you shall return to calm,
as the river finds its way,
or the bloom its opening.

So grow,
not in fear of the winds
but in the stillness
that follows rain—
and let your heart be as wide

as the sky above,
full of wonder,
without end.

15. You Were Water

In the days I sank lowest,
you didn't reach in with noise
or declarations.
You stayed—
as if staying were a kind of knowing.

You said nothing
of strength or hope.
No urging toward the light.
Only your presence,
unmoving,
like water seeping into dry stone.

I had come undone—
edges softened,
colours dulled,
tired of being seen.
But you didn't flinch.
You held the space,
made room for what I couldn't speak.

You reminded me,

without saying it,
that even the broken
can root again.
That stillness needn't mean surrender.

You were water—
unassuming,
unremarkable,
and utterly essential.

16. Big and Little

As kids, we loved the little things—
A skipping stone, the swing's soft swing,
The rustle of the monsoon breeze,
The magic found in climbing trees.

A sticker star, a secret note,
The paper boats we used to float,
A giggle in the pouring rain,
A Band-Aid kiss to ease the pain.

We marveled at the firefly's gleam,
Spun worlds from just a midnight dream,
Our pockets full of stones and sand,
Believing wishes made by hand.

But now we chase the grander prize—
The house, the car, the painted skies,
A love that burns instead of glows,
The kind the world applauds and knows.

Yet somewhere in this grown-up race,
We miss the joy, the gentle grace—
Of laughing till we couldn't breathe,

Of love that didn't need to leave.

So may we pause, remember when
The little things were all we had—
And all we needed, even then.

17. "Like Water, My Love"

It started soft, the way I feel—
A quiet stream, intense but real.
It touched the edges of my soul,
Then slipped away to stay whole.

It lingered warm, but wouldn't wait,
Too honest to negotiate.
It wants to stay but can't—it knows,
It needs to breathe, it needs to flow.

I don't hold tight, I let it be,
This love that moves so wild in me.
And deep inside, I always know—
What's meant returns, like rivers grow.

18. Doe-Eyed

A hush in the shape of dusk,
where your gaze begins.
Soft edges blur—
not quite sorrow, not quite sky.

Thoughts flicker
like shadows through water,
unspoken,
but echoing loud
in the stillness between blinks.

You look,
and time folds.
You don't ask to be known—
yet there you are,
etched
in the corners of every quiet.

Warm gravity.
A question.
The pause between heartbeat and breath.
Big, wide,
unanswerable eyes.

19. The Freedom to Eat

I sit. I slice. I pour, I chew—
not hurried, not ashamed, not new.
But something in this bite feels bold,
a quiet war that's long grown old.

No tally kept, no voices near,
just me, and warmth, and something clear:
this is my choice—this plate, this peace,
a soft revolt, a rich release.

The butter melts, the gravy sings,
the bread forgives the tighter things.
What once was weighed now simply *is*,
a moment mine, a mouthful bliss.

Let others shrink to fit their form—
I'll take the fire, I'll keep the warm.
For in this fullness, slow and sweet,
I find myself,
complete.

20. Liberation From Thyself

I shed the skin that wasn't mine,
freed myself from all the "shoulds."
No longer bound by old ideals,
I stand—wild, whole, and true.

No longer the version they expected,
no longer the one I thought I had to be.
In this moment, I am simply me,
alive,
free.